1979

MASTER PAINTERS
OF HOLLAND

MASTER PAINTERS OF HOLLAND

Dutch painting in the seventeenth century

Herbert Wiesner

EXCALIBUR BOOKS

Excalibur Books, 201 Park Avenue South, New York, N.Y. 10003
©1976 Elsevier Publishing Projects SA, Lausanne
English language edition ©1976 by Phaidon Press Limited, Oxford.
ISBN 0–525–70056–0
Library of Congress Catalog Card Number: 76–21957
Printed in Italy by Amilcare Pizzi SpA, Milan

Master Painters of Holland

The seventeenth century in the Netherlands was one of the richest periods in the history of art. After years of struggle against Spanish domination, the northern provinces won their independence in 1609. The tremendous industrial and commercial activity that followed made Holland one of the most important and powerful countries in the world. At the same time there was an extraordinary outburst of artistic talent: the great wealth and national pride stimulated a new generation of artists, and the prosperous middle class provided a market for works of art. There was demand for art that was down to earth and true to nature, and the artists responded. In this competitive atmosphere the Dutch artists tended to specialize. Hercules Seghers, Jan van Goyen, Aelbert Cuyp, Jacob van Ruisdael and Meyndert Hobbema painted landscapes; Pieter de Hoogh and Gerard ter Borch excelled in interiors; Adriaen Brouwer, Adriaen van Ostade and Jan Steen painted scenes of contemporary life; Willem Kalf concentrated on still lifes; Jan van de Cappelle and Willem van de Velde devoted themselves to marine painting. The greatest of the Dutch masters were Frans Hals, who brought portraiture to a new height; Johannes Vermeer, remembered for his lovely young women and exquisite interiors; and Rembrandt, the versatile genius. It is on these three masters that this brief survey concentrates.

The portraitist Frans Hals came from a Protestant Flemish family. He was probably born about 1580 in Antwerp, but from 1585 onwards he lived in Holland. We have little information about his life, but it is known that he became a respected citizen of the town of Haarlem. In 1610 he joined the painters' guild, the Guild of St Luke, and in 1644 he was elected to serve on its governing body. Although he had never been short of public or private commissions, his financial position grew ever more precarious and in his old age he incurred debts simply to pay for daily necessities. At last, two years before his death in August 1666, the town council of Haarlem awarded him a pension: it was not so much a charitable gift as recognition of the high regard in which he was held.

Hals is believed to have been a pupil of the mannerist painter and art historian Karel van Mander, whose style was based on that of the Italian masters. But so little is known of Hals's early work that his artistic training cannot be reliably ascertained. The *Banquet in a Park* (formerly in the Berlin Museum; destroyed in 1945), which was probably one of his early paintings, showed a peasant wedding still somewhat in the tradition of Pieter Bruegel and also of Karel van Mander. It has little in common with his later paintings—well over two hundred of his portraits are known—with their bold, rapid brushwork.

The first major commission he carried out was the *Banquet of the Officers of the St George Militia Company* (Haarlem, Frans Hals Museum), painted in 1616. It shows the traditional farewell banquet of the civic guard officers who had served from 1612 to 1615. The composition of such official commemorative pictures was subject to long-established conventions, but Hals, who had known the officers during his own militia service, succeeded in giving this group portrait a quite distinctive character. The arrangement of the banqueters, which is somewhat influenced by pictorial representations of Christ's Last Supper with the Apostles, the seemingly effortless division of the whole into smaller groups, and the feeling of zest and well-being which pervades the scene, reveal a noticeable originality. Hals's early paintings are characterized by heavy local colours, rather drily applied, which lack the sparkling brightness of his middle period. Another early work, the *Shrovetide Revellers* (New York, Metropolitan Museum of Art), may lack the final touches: it is rather cramped in composition, and whereas the figures in the foreground are carefully finished, the background has remained rather sketchy. In the 1620s Hals was to concentrate on genre pictures of this type. Among them are the *Laughing Boy with a Jug* (Plate 7), the *Drinking Boy* and the *Boy Holding a Flute* (Schwerin, Staatliches Museum), the various versions of fisherboys and fishergirls (one of them formerly in the Brooklyn Museum, New York) and, above all, the *Merry Drinker* (Amsterdam, Rijksmuseum) and, slightly later, the *Gipsy Girl* (Plate 8).

During this decade Hals's technique was changing: the dry, heavy colouring gives way to a lighter, richer tonal range, and the distinctly visible, seemingly spontaneous brushstrokes now model each object in such a convincingly lifelike manner that he has sometimes been regarded as a forerunner of the French Impressionists. This may account, to some extent, for the great fame he came to enjoy in the later nineteenth century. The development of his individual style—which must be seen within the context of Baroque painting as a whole—can be discerned in the infectiously joyful picture of *Jonker Ramp and his Sweetheart* of 1623 (Plate 10). Among the most important paintings of the middle period are the *Banquet of the Officers of the St Hadrian Militia Company* (Plates 11,46) and the second *Banquet of the Officers of the St George Militia Company* (Plates 12, 47). In comparison with the militia portrait of 1616 the sitters are now more clearly differentiated, each of them revealing, as it were, the innermost core of his personality. These paintings seem to vibrate with colourful life and diversity.

In the 1630s another change of style can be detected. The artist begins to lose interest in popular, realistic genre subjects, while the expression of his sitters becomes more serious and composed. This development runs parallel with an increasing concentration on essentials and, probably under the influence of Rembrandt, a quieter, more harmonious colouring. Good examples of this phase are the noble portraits of *Nicolaes van der Meer* and his wife, *Cornelia Vooght* (Haarlem, Frans Hals Museum). Similar tendencies can be found in the great group portraits of this period, the *Officers and Sergeants of the St Hadrian Militia Company* (Haarlem, Frans Hals Museum), the *Corporalship of Captain Reynier Reael and Lieutenant Cornelis Michielsz. Blaeuw* (Amsterdam, Rijksmuseum) and the *Officers and Sergeants of the St George Militia Company* (Haarlem, Frans Hals Museum). The two group portraits in Haarlem are set in the open air: man is placed in relation to nature, but the landscape remains subordinate.

The tendency towards simplification and restraint continues in the 1640s. Instead of militia groups Hals now portrays governors of the social institutions in Haarlem. In 1641 he painted the *Regents of the St Elizabeth Hospital* (Haarlem, Frans Hals Museum) and if we compare this to the civic guard portraits we notice immediately how the smaller number of sitters results in greater tranquillity, which is brought about by an economy of pictorial means. Two colours, black and white, are combined in a harmonious, consistent tone of silvery grey. The influence of the painters of Amsterdam, particularly Rembrandt, can be detected. But Hals had not stopped experimenting: the lively portrait of *Willem van Heythuyzen* tilting his chair (Plate 9), probably completed at the end of the 1630s, might have been painted during an informal chat.

In Hals's late period the brushwork becomes ever freer and lighter. A sitter's hands, face and sleeves are often summarily indicated with sweeping strokes of the brush. The portrait of *Vincent Laurensz. van der Vinne* (Toronto, Art Gallery) is a good example of a penetrating likeness achieved with a minimum of technical means. The same is true of the two group portraits painted in 1664, the *Regents of the Old Men's Alms House* (Plate 23) and the *Regentesses of the Old Men's Alms House* (Haarlem, Frans Hals Museum). At one time it was thought that one of the Regents was shown as a drunkard and that the women's faces betrayed meanness and cruelty, but however bitter or critical the aged master may have been it is hardly credible that he intended to make his sitters appear ridiculous. What is more likely is that he had a deep insight into the darker aspects of old age. The composition is even more restrained than previously, the figures appear to be isolated rather than parts of a group. The painter's attention is wholly devoted to the facial features and the expressive hands.

Like many Haarlem artists, Hals had a considerable number of pupils. Among them were—in addition to his sons—Judith Leyster; Jan Molenaer; Adriaen Brouwer, whose technique, especially in his small genre pictures (Plates 41, 71), was closest to that of Hals; and Adriaen van Ostade, who concentrated on small-scale scenes of peasant life (Plate 61) painted in a detailed style. Genre pictures reached their height with an artist from Leyden, Jan Steen, who was one of the greatest artists of the century. In the 1660s Steen lived in Haarlem, where he joined the painters' guild and where he discovered the work of Hals. His humorous scenes of low and middle-class life, which reveal his extraordinary genius as a painter and a draughtsman, are not only comic but often have underlying moral lessons to impart. That the paintings can be enjoyed on both levels is a testament to the comic ingenuity and invention of Jan Steen.

Hals's art of portraiture had no direct successors, although an artist thought to have been a pupil of his, Johannes Verspronck, became a successful portrait painter (Plate 54). It can, however, be traced in later times. What gave him great historical importance was, above all, that he broke away from the influence of the south and established a Dutch school of painting that was independent of Italian models. Soon after his death his pictures began to be neglected, but for that very reason the enthusiasm for them was all the greater when he was rediscovered in the nineteenth century, and since then he has enjoyed continuous popularity. In the present century the view of his work has somewhat changed. Whereas the Impressionists, fascinated by the freshness and spontaneity of his technique, hailed Hals as one of their forefathers, more recent critics tend to pay more attention to the rational, geometric elements of his compositional style and to place his work in the intellectual and visual context of the Baroque as a whole.

If Hals was one of the founders of the national Dutch school of painting, the pictures of Johannes Vermeer lifted Dutch everyday life on to a level of classic, monumental greatness. Like Hals, Vermeer seems to have worked exclusively as a painter in oils, and again like him he took most of his subjects from the middle-class world around him. And finally he shared with Hals the fate of being almost completely forgotten for two hundred years, until he was rediscovered in France during the nineteenth century. In 1866 a French art critic, Théophile Bürger-Thoré, published three articles in the Gazette des Beaux-Arts which laid the basis for the modern appreciation of Vermeer's art. It was again the Impressionists who helped to establish the master's enduring fame although they admired the work of Vermeer and that of Hals for quite different reasons.

Vermeer was born in 1632 in Delft, where his father, also a native of Delft, kept an inn, besides working as an art-dealer and silk-weaver. In 1653 the painter married Catharina Bolnes, a Catholic; in the same year he joined the painters' guild, and in 1662–3 and 1669–70 he served as a member of the guild's governing body. After his father's death in 1655, he took over the house and continued to run the dealer's shop for the rest of his life. It was not unusual for Dutch artists of that time to practise a trade, and dealing in works of art was an obvious choice. Rembrandt, too, carried on such a business, and Jan Steen ran a brewery in Delft in the 1650s. It seems that Vermeer was more successful in selling the work of other painters than his own, for on his death in 1675 his widow inherited 29 of his pictures, more than half his entire output. It is also significant that three pictures came into the possession of a baker, to whom the artist owed money. Although Vermeer had a reputation as an art expert—he was called in as a valuer in a scandalous international transaction with the Elector of Brandenburg—his business was far from prosperous, probably in part because those were the years when Louis XIV of France was waging war against the Dutch Republic.

We know little about Vermeer's early artistic training. When he began his apprenticeship, about 1647, the Delft school of painting was relatively unimportant. He may have been taught by Leonard Bramer (who some years later was a witness to his marriage), or, perhaps more probably, by Hendrick van der Burgh, but we have no evidence. Carel Fabritius, who is sometimes described as his teacher, did not come to Delft until 1650 and joined the painters' guild there barely one year before Vermeer. When Fabritius, Paulus Potter, Pieter de Hoogh and Jan Steen settled in Delft, the local school came into its own, with Vermeer its central figure.

Continuing an earlier local tradition of architectural compositions, the Delft painters specialized in the study of perspective, and some of them, particularly Fabritius, in *trompe-l'oeil* painting. Perspective views from one room into the next owed their popularity mainly to Samuel van Hoogstraten, who had been, like Fabritius, a pupil of Rembrandt. In developing these studies the painters made use of technical aids, including the camera obscura, which had become widely known in the later sixteenth century and which led to strangely cool, almost surrealist visual effects. The use of such scientific devices may have been encouraged by Antony van Leeuwenhoek, the Delft naturalist, who ground his own lenses and combined them in microscopes to pursue his wide-ranging discoveries. It seems quite likely that Vermeer was acquainted with him. A pronounced interest in the interaction of light and colour also suggests that the painters of Delft, and Vermeer in particular, had a gift for exact observation that almost matched that of the scientists.

Vermeer's earliest dated work, the *Procuress* of 1656 (Plate 92), shows affinities with the works of Dirck van Baburen, Gerrit van Honthorst and Hendrick ter Brugghen (Plate 38), but the warmer colouring also recalls Rembrandt or Italian models such as Caravaggio. The draped barrier in the foreground, which creates an impression of distance between the spectator and the sitters, was also an invention of Italian painters; it can be found again in later paintings by Vermeer. The head at the left may well be a self-portrait of the artist. A similar dense application of paint and cramped composition characterize two other early pictures, *Christ in the House of Mary and Martha* (Plate 86), and *Diana with her Companions* (The Hague, Mauritshuis), both of which depict subjects that were not to recur in Vermeer's later work. The mythological painting has affinities with a painting by Jacob van Loo (formerly in the Berlin Museum; destroyed in the Second World War), while the picture of Christ is a variation of a type that was then common throughout European art.

Another early work is the *Sleeping Girl* of 1656 (New York, Metropolitan Museum of Art). Here nearly half the foreground is filled by a table decorated with rugs and a carefully arranged still life, and by a chair placed at an angle. The sitter seems to be almost hemmed in between the table and the wall at the back, but next to her the view is extended: an open door affords a glimpse into the adjoining room. In a seventeenth-century sale catalogue the girl is said to have fallen asleep because she is drunk. It seems more relevant to ask why she should be so sorrowful and melancholy: perhaps it is because of an unhappy love affair, to which the picture of Cupid in the background may also allude.

One of Vermeer's first true masterpieces is the *Soldier and Laughing Girl* (New York, Frick Collection). Though the picture falls short of the clarity of his later work, the girl with her enchanting smile, set before a light background, is already typical of the artist's mature style. The *Lady Reading a Letter at an Open Window* (Plate 33) dates from the same period. The window, the chair and even the dress are familiar to us from the previous picture, but now the sitter, intensely concentrating on what she is reading, is placed within a framework of curtains, window and draped table. This spatial composition anticipates many of Vermeer's later paintings, while the treatment of light, with the tiny glittering dots on the carpet, shows that he had learned to dispense with the strong contrasts of light and dark derived from the school of Caravaggio. The illusionist reflection of the girl in the open window is a device that was later to be taken over by Gabriel Metsu. Soon afterwards Vermeer achieved a better balance between space and figure in the almost statuesque *Servant Girl Pouring Milk* (Plate 31), which is perhaps the most popular of his pictures. The table, placed diagonally in the room, clarifies the scene, which is depicted with an almost photographic accuracy, and the light reflections play around the bright, truly monumental figure of the girl.

Nearly all the scenes which Vermeer depicted are set in the confined space of his studio, but we have two pictures of outdoor views: the *View of Delft* (Plate 6), a homage to his native city, and the *Street in Delft* (Plate 77), which shows us what he saw when he looked out of the window. (A third picture of the town has been lost.) It seems that he simply opened the window which appears at the left in many of his pictures and that he steadily observed the old people's home across the street. There is nothing exciting or deliberate in the composition: the profoundly tranquil scene, owing its magic solely to the light, to the colours and to the way it is cut by the frame, is enlivened less by the figures than by the small irregularities in the brick walls. It is this calm and restraint that distinguishes Vermeer's picture from the busy street scenes painted by masters such as Pieter de Hoogh.

If the *Street in Delft* seems relatively flat, the much larger *View of Delft* is of considerable spatial depth—an impression aided by the subtle colour modulations and the skilfully blurred reflections on the water. The seemingly three-dimensional vault of heaven above the townscape fills nearly half of the canvas. This picture, too, conveys an impression of contemplative serenity, and the few figures in the foreground serve to articulate the composition rather than to introduce an element of stage design.

The pictures which Vermeer painted in the 1660s are generally regarded as his most precious and perfect works. Blue, yellow and sometimes red have now become dominant, the colours are lighter in tone, the light is cool, almost artificial, and the play of the shadows is used sparingly. The figures are placed within a tight framework made up of the most diverse objects. The use which Vermeer made of light and colour to create space and depth in the *View of Delft* is also the secret of the *Girl with a Wineglass* (Brunswick, Herzog Anton Ulrich Museum), unfortunately badly preserved, and the *Woman in Blue Reading a Letter* (Amsterdam, Rijksmuseum), whose marvellously blue maternity smock reflects the light from a window that is not visible. Closely related to this picture is the *Young Lady with a Pearl Necklace* (Plate 34). The posture of Vermeer's models and his arrangement of the furnishings vary surprisingly little, but the young woman's gaze scrutinizing her appearance, not without a hint of vanity, gives this picture a special accent and implies a relation between tangible ornament and beauty of mind. In another picture of that time, the *Lady Weighing Pearls* (Plate 32), the greater seriousness of expression hints at a similar significance, but the Last Judgement on the wall behind her, a picture within a picture, suggests even deeper levels of meaning: an analogy between the weighing of pearls and the weighing of virtuous and sinful souls on the Day of Judgement. This interpretation also lends the mirror a deeper significance as a symbol of the vanity of all earthly things.

About 1666 Vermeer painted the *Painter in his Studio* (Plate 82), a famous allegorical picture, which passed after his death into the possession of his wife's mother. This work, with its use of pure perspective and strong contrasts, marks the beginning of his final period. The anonymous painter, seen from the back, is no longer a dark foreground figure, but a black and white contrast in the middleground, whereas the foreground remains almost empty, a device which makes the room appear very large. The girl who poses as the painter's model has been variously interpreted: formerly she was thought to personify Fame, the allegory of glory, but today she is often identified as Clio, the Muse of History, holding the trumpet of fame in her right hand and the chronicle of world events in her left. If she is Clio, then the objects on the table, one of them a mask, would be the attributes of the other Muses, and the painter himself a narrator of stories or of history. But he is shown painting the model's laurel wreath, perhaps after all an allusion to the fame that posterity may have in store for him. The face and pose of the 'Muse' call to mind another of Vermeer's pictures, the *Girl with Pearl Eardrops* (The Hague, Mauritshuis).

The *Astronomer* (Plate 35) and the *Geographer* (Frankfurt, Städelsches Kunstinstitut), dating from the late 1660s, have much in common. Their interpretation depends on whether they were in fact intended to hang side by side as companion pieces. If that is so, then they may be regarded as metaphorical representations of heavenly and earthly life. But it is by no means certain that the man in the second picture is a geographer since he leans over a map of the stars and a celestial globe stands on the cupboard behind him. These accessories might lead the spectator to interpret the picture as an allegory of the religious life on earth.

Among the most important of Vermeer's late paintings are the *Lady Writing a Letter, with her Maid* (Ireland, Private Collection) and the *Young Woman Standing at a Virginal* (London, National Gallery), which also provide excellent examples of pictures within pictures. The Cupid and the musical instrument in the London picture are allusions to some love affair. Both paintings are masterly in their compositional balance. The daylight, which seems diffused as through a filter, fills the whole of the room and creates an unreal atmosphere.

The *Allegory of Faith* (New York, Metropolitan Museum of Art), one of Vermeer's last paintings, has never found many admirers. Although perfect in its details, it leaves the beholder cold. It was probably painted on commission and was based on a literary source which cramped the artist's imagination. Here, once again, there is a picture within a picture: Christ on the Cross by Jacob Jordaens.

Vermeer's oeuvre is easy to survey, not only because it is small in quantity, but also because the figure motifs and accessories are frequently repeated. He excelled less in invention than in the rendering of light and in subtle colour harmonies. That may have been the reason why, as mentioned earlier, it was the French Impressionists who rediscovered him. They can hardly have been impressed by his handling of the brush, for it was quite unlike the bold, spontaneous brushwork of Hals, which they admired so greatly. Vermeer applied his paints until he had achieved a perfect and brilliant smoothness and no trace was left of any manual effort. What his discoverers admired were his pointillist effects and the magical luminosity of his art.

Although the quality of Vermeer's art sets him apart, he was in fact only one of a number of painters of the domestic interior. Pieter de Hoogh, Gerard ter Borch, Gabriel Metsu and Gerrit Dou are all worthy of serious consideration in any account of Dutch painting. De Hoogh's best works date from his years in Delft (about 1653 to 1662) and suggest some influence from Vermeer in their spatial clarity and careful observation of light (Plates 56, 83). However, de Hoogh was neither as technically gifted nor as rigorous as Vermeer; the lighting, though very well managed, is never quite as clear or accurate and the feeling for space is without the scrupulous delicacy of his great contemporary.

Gerard ter Borch was a remarkably good portrait painter, and his heads, invariably painted on a small, almost miniature scale, have the gravity and sharpness of insight that put them on a level with Samuel Cooper, the greatest portrait miniaturist of the century. But ter Borch is much better known for his scenes of elegant life (Plates 57, 72, 88), which, in spite of their sometimes ostentatious skill, evident in the handling of satin for which he was famous, and contrary to their occasionally erotic undertones, have a seriousness and tenderness that is all the more pleasing for being somewhat unexpected. Ter Borch, at his best, foreshadows the complexity of Watteau in *his* scenes of gallantry.

Gabriel Metsu is a less interesting painter, who died relatively young. His usual subject matter is much the same as that of de Hoogh, Vermeer and ter Borch and at his finest reveals a comparable alliance of technical skill and observation. The *Sick Child* (Plate 89) is unusual for Metsu in its direct appeal to our sympathies; but it is saved from mawkishness by virtue of its simplicity and tact—neither mother nor child, for example, looks at the spectator. The image of the Crucifixion on the wall behind suggests the seventeenth-century religious context in which this type of painting would have been unconsciously judged.

Gerrit Dou, who began as a pupil of Rembrandt, quickly evolved into a master of highly finished cabinet pictures (Plate 63) that earned him a European reputation. Charles II pleaded in vain with him to come to England; and his works were greatly admired by Queen Christina of Sweden.

Rembrandt Harmensz. van Rijn was the greatest Dutch painter, and he is also the only one who is now counted unreservedly among the greatest artists of all time. He achieved a unique mastery in oil painting, in drawing with pen and chalks, and in etching on copper plates, and his choice of subjects comprised an enormous range. As a result his oeuvre as a whole is of greater depth and variety than that of any other painter working north of the Alps. And yet Rembrandt, like Hals and Vermeer, was long forgotten, even rejected. Once again it was in France that the ground was prepared for the modern appreciation of his achievement. In 1851 the painter Eugene Delacroix noted in his diary: 'Perhaps it will be found that Rembrandt is a much greater painter than Raphael', but his *Journals* were not published until the last decade of the nineteenth century.

Rembrandt was born in Leyden in 1606, the son of a miller and a baker's daughter. The family was named 'van Rijn' because their mill stood near the bank of the Old Rhine. Rembrandt's parents intended him for a learned profession and enrolled him in the Latin school and, in 1620, in the University of Leyden, then one of the most famous in Europe. But he soon followed his real bent and became an apprentice to an insignificant local painter, Jacob van Swanenburgh, a late follower of Hieronymus Bosch. His artistic training did not begin in earnest until 1623, when he studied in Amsterdam under the famous history painter Pieter Lastman. After six months he returned to Leyden and soon set up his first studio. In 1631 he left his native city and settled permanently in Amsterdam. In his six or seven working years in Leyden, when he had already a gifted pupil (Gerrit Dou), his art attained a range of development that might have fulfilled the aspirations of many a modest painter.

His earliest paintings reveal the influence of Lastman both in colour and design, and above all in the choice of subject. Even before he became apprenticed to Lastman he had probably read the critical writings of Karel van Mander, which were largely based on Italian art theory, and had turned away from the popular realistic themes typical of Dutch painting, such as still life, genre scenes and portraits. The preference for such everyday subjects, so conspicuous in the work of Hals and Vermeer, reminds us that the Protestant Church in Holland was hostile to religious imagery and condemned the representation of saints as idolatrous superstition, while the educated nobility was not numerous enough to create a steady demand for allegorical, mythological or historical pictures. Hence Rembrandt's decision to follow in the steps of Lastman, a painter trained in the Italian tradition, especially that of Caravaggio, ran counter to the direction which Dutch art had taken.

His style soon freed itself from dependence on that of Lastman, and for what he still lacked in technical accomplishment he made up by psychological penetration. In the *Stoning of St Stephen* (Lyons, Musée des Beaux-Arts), painted when he was twenty years old, he depicted the martyr's agony and ecstasy with a depth of expression that distinguished the picture from Lastman's somewhat rhetorical compositions. It was also in his Leyden period, and perhaps in this very picture, that he began his great series of self-portraits. They have little resemblance to one another, since he simply studied various expressions in order to deepen his psychological understanding. He depicted his own features in well over one hundred drawings, etchings and paintings, and so created a visual autobiography with all the artistic means at his command. He also made portraits of his parents, among which is one of his mother now in the Royal Collection (Plate 42).

In 1631 Rembrandt took the decisive step of moving to the prosperous city of Amsterdam, where he lived in the house of the rich art-dealer Hendrick van Uylenburgh. Here he met Hendrick's niece, Saskia, a charming, well-to-do girl whom he married in 1634. He had already established a reputation as a painter and Saskia's wealth enabled him to set up house in comfort.

Fame had come to him in 1632 almost overnight with the *Anatomy Lesson of Dr Tulp* (Plate 25), a picture of seven men, dressed in dark costumes with white ruffs, grouped round a corpse and Professor Nicolaes Tulp, who demonstrates the muscles of the arm. As the picture was a commission, each of the men had to be clearly visible. Rembrandt solved the compositional problem by grouping the eight participants in a flat pyramid, behind and beside the diagonally placed corpse. Their attention is skilfully differentiated: some are looking at the lecturer, some at the dissected arm, and others at an anatomy atlas lying open in the foreground. Thomas de Keyser and Nicolaes Eliasz., both of whom had also competed for this commission, would have produced a drily descriptive guild portrait; Rembrandt's chiaroscuro, reminiscent of Caravaggio, gives the scene an exciting life of its own.

During the following decade Rembrandt became unquestionably the most fashionable portraitist and teacher in Amsterdam. His prosperity increased with his fame, and so did his eagerness to bring together an art collection that would rival those of the merchants trading with distant shores. He developed a veritable passion for amassing works of art, precious stones, cloths and textiles, many of which later served as accessories in his pictures. But such was his expenditure on these luxuries that by 1639, when he moved into a new house (the present Rembrandt Museum), he was in debt.

Although he had a steady stream of portrait commissions he had enough time to devote himself to what interested him most—subjects taken from the Old and New Testaments. Constantijn Huygens, secretary to Prince Frederick Henry of Orange, Stadholder of the United Dutch Provinces, had obtained for him a commission for a series depicting the Passion of Christ. These pictures, which are now in the Alte Pinakothek in Munich, were begun about 1633. The *Raising of the Cross*, painted after the *Descent of the Cross*, clearly shows Rembrandt's reaction to the Baroque style of Rubens, whose pictures of these two subjects were probably familiar to him from engravings. Whereas Rubens had depicted Christ as a heroic figure, Rembrandt, in a more austere interpretation of the *Raising*, emphasizes the crucified Saviour's frailty and helplessness. Moreover, he gave one of the bystanders his own features, probably as a token of humility and as an acknowledgement that he knew himself to be a sinner.

It was natural that he felt a need to respond to the work of Rubens, who was universally renowned as the prince of painters. Some of Rembrandt's pictures betray even a direct influence, for instance an early *Holy Family* (Munich, Alte Pinakothek), where the Virgin recalls the buxom women of the Flemish master, or the *Blinding of Samson* (Frankfurt, Städelsches Kunstinstitut), which he sent as a gift to Constantijn Huygens.

The completion of the remaining pictures of the Passion series now became urgent. In 1636 Rembrandt painted the *Ascension of Christ*, but the *Resurrection* and the *Entombment* were not delivered until three years later. In January 1639 he wrote to Huygens that he had expressed in the pictures 'the greatest and most natural emotion'. Although the composition of the *Entombment* is indeed rather calm, the *Wedding of Samson* of 1638 (Dresden, Gemäldegalerie) shows how much, in general, Rembrandt tended to dramatize an event and to choose its most vehement moment. The groups of the wedding guests seem to split asunder with a centrifugal movement, while Delilah is enthroned in the centre, as cold and fateful as a sphinx.

A *Self-Portrait* of 1640 (London, National Gallery) seems to mark the conclusion of this happy time in Rembrandt's life. Based on Raphael's portrait of Baldassare Castiglione, which he had seen in the previous year, it shows him as a man proud of his success and dressed in a theatrical costume. But the sceptical, questioning glance reveals greater depth: it seems to hint at a change in the artist's self-awareness and even to suggest a presentiment of the blows which fate had in store for him.

The year 1642 was a decisive one in Rembrandt's life. First he completed his largest surviving picture, the *Militia Company of Captain Frans Banning Cocq* (Plate 55). It was named the 'Night Watch' much later, when it had darkened considerably, but it has now been cleaned and shows once again the original daylight scene. Today the '*Night Watch*' is perhaps Rembrandt's most popular picture, but the men portrayed were greatly disappointed. To understand their feelings we must remember that this is not a record of a militia company suddenly marching out at night, but a posed portrait of the civic guard assembling in high spirits under their captain, Frans Banning Cocq, and their lieutenant, Willem van Ruytenburgh. As each of the men paid his share towards the picture, they felt justified in expecting formal portraits, such as those in the militia groups painted by Frans Hals. Rembrandt gave them instead a dramatic crowd scene worthy of Shakespeare. What looks at first sight like the vision of a magnificent tumult is in fact a carefully balanced arrangement of figure groups and rhythmic light gradations. Portrayed in this novel manner, the militiamen may well have failed to appreciate the originality of this masterpiece; but the tradition that a scandal ensued is now discredited as a romantic fabrication.

1 *Esaias van de Velde.* A Winter Scene. *1614. Raleigh, North Carolina, Museum of Art*

2 *Jan van Goyen.* Landscape with a Tavern. *1646. Paris, Musée du Petit-Palais*

3 *Pieter Saenredam*. Old Town Hall, Amsterdam. *1657. Amsterdam, Rijksmuseum*

4 *Jan van der Heyden*. New Town Hall, Amsterdam. *Paris, Louvre*

5 *Gerrit Berckheyde*. The Flower Market in Amsterdam. *Amsterdam, Rijksmuseum*

6 *Johannes Vermeer*. View of Delft. *About 1660. The Hague, Mauritshuis*

7 *Frans Hals*. Laughing Boy with a Jug. *1626–8. Rotterdam, Boymans–van Beuningen Museum*

8 *Frans Hals*. Gipsy Girl. *About 1628–30. Paris, Louvre*

9 *Frans Hals*. Willem van Heythuyzen. *About 1637–9. Brussels, Musée Royal des Beaux-Arts*

10 *Frans Hals*. Jonker Ramp and his Sweetheart. *1623. New York, Metropolitan Museum of Art*

11 *Frans Hals*. Banquet of the Officers of the St Hadrian Militia Company. *About 1627. Haarlem, Frans Hals Museum*

12 *Frans Hals*. Banquet of the Officers of the St George Militia Company. *About 1627. Haarlem, Frans Hals Museum*

13 *Salomon van Ruysdael.* Coast with Fishcarts. *1635(?). Whereabouts unknown*

14 *Simon de Vlieger.* Beach near Scheveningen. *1633. Greenwich, National Maritime Museum*

15 *Allart van Everdingen*. Snowstorm at Sea. *Chantilly, Musée Condé*

16 *Aert van der Neer.* Frozen River. *Amsterdam, Rijksmuseum*

17 *Jan van de Cappelle.* Bridge across a Frozen Canal. *1653. The Hague, Mauritshuis*

18 *Paulus Potter.* Cows Reflected in the Water. *1648. The Hague, Mauritshuis*

19 *Aelbert Cuyp.* The Avenue at Meerdervoort, Dordrecht. *About 1660–5. London, Wallace Collection*

20 *Jan Steen*. Grace before Meat. *About 1665. London, National Gallery*

21 *Jan Steen.* The Dissolute Family. *Private Collection*

22 *Rembrandt.* The Sampling Officials of the Clothmakers' Guild, Amsterdam ('The Syndics'). *1661/2. Amsterdam, Rijksmuseum*

23 *Frans Hals.* Regents of the Old Men's Alms House. *About 1664. Haarlem, Frans Hals Museum*

24 *Rembrandt*. Portrait of Jan Six. *1654.*
Amsterdam, Six Collection

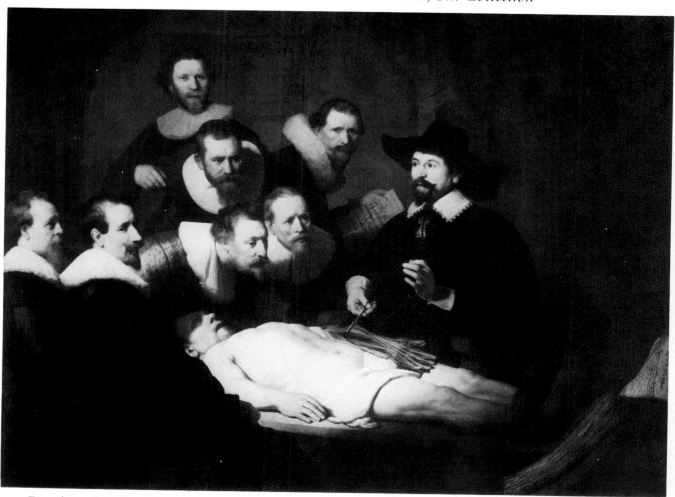

25 *Rembrandt*. The Anatomy Lesson of Dr Nicolaes Tulp. *1632. The Hague, Mauritshuis*

26 *Rembrandt*. The Jewish Bride. *After 1665. Amsterdam, Rijksmuseum*

27 *Rembrandt.* The Return of the Prodigal Son. *About 1668–9. Leningrad, Hermitage*

28 *Jacob van Ruisdael*. Castle of Bentheim. *Amsterdam, Rijksmuseum*

29 *Jacob van Ruisdael*. A Landscape with a Ruined Castle and a Church. *London, National Gallery*

30 *Meyndert Hobbema*. The Ruins of Brederode Castle. *1671. London, National Gallery*

31 *Johannes Vermeer*. Servant Girl Pouring Milk.
   About 1660. Amsterdam, Rijksmuseum

32 *Johannes Vermeer*. Lady Weighing Pearls.
   About 1665. Washington, National Gallery of Art

33 *Johannes Vermeer*. Lady Reading a Letter at
an Open Window. *About 1658. Dresden,
Gemäldegalerie*

34 *Johannes Vermeer*. Young Lady with a Pearl
Necklace. *About 1665. Berlin-Dahlem, Staatliche
Museen*

35 *Johannes Vermeer*. The Astronomer. *1668. Paris, Private Collection*

36 *Carel Fabritius. A Goldfinch. 1654. The Hague, Mauritshuis*

But Rembrandt began to receive fewer portrait commissions, probably because fashion was changing and his dark, atmospheric manner found less favour than the work of Bartholomeus van der Helst, who was working in the style of Anthony van Dyck. Even Rembrandt's pupils adapted themselves to that style, but the master himself, in spite of his misfortunes, did not lose his self-confidence. Financial troubles could no longer cause him serious concern, let alone make him change his dark palette or his uncompromising style.

Another crucial event of 1642 was the death of his wife, shortly after the birth of her son, Titus. The grieving master commemorated her once more, in a posthumous portrait, and then he seems to have moved to the countryside, for it was in that period that he made his few pure studies of landscape.

In the 1640s he painted some impressively calm or even oppressively silent pictures, among them the *Holy Family in the Carpenter's Workshop* (Leningrad, Hermitage) and the *Adoration of the Shepherds* (Munich, Alte Pinakothek), where the concern of the parents and shepherds for the sleeping child is almost palpable. In those years Rembrandt fell in love with Hendrickje Stoffels, who was to keep house for him until the end of her life, but was unable to stem the tide of financial disaster. In 1656 he was declared bankrupt and two years later he was forced to sell off his possessions. He had to part with seventy of his own pictures as well as with his house and art treasures. The catalogue of that sale provides interesting information about his collections. From then onwards Rembrandt was financially dependent on Hendrickje and his son Titus; they opened an art-dealer's business and employed him as an expert.

Hendrickje posed as model for many of his pictures which combined portraiture with an historical theme. In 1654 she had borne him a daughter, and in the same year he painted her as *Bathsheba with King David's Letter* (Plate 87)—at once an Old Testament scene and a portrait of a woman lost in thought and meditating on a letter which she has just received. The warm flesh tones of the body are reminiscent of the nudes of Titian.

Rembrandt often chose subjects that surprised his contemporaries. The picture of *Jacob Blessing the Children of Joseph* (Kassel, Gemäldegalerie) lacks both movement (which would have appealed to the admirers of the Baroque style) and an obvious moral message (which would have pleased the classicists). It takes for its underlying theme the mysterious designs of God and the peace that comes from co-operation with the Divine will. But ultimately it simply tells us of the bond of love which joins the members of the family.

The *Portrait of Jan Six* (Plate 24), painted in 1654, can be regarded as representative of the portraits of that decade. Rembrandt shows us his friend's thoughtful, questioning gaze; the right hand holds the glove, and the red coat, draped over one shoulder, is the strongest colour accent among the grey tones dominating the picture. But these greys were not pigments on the artist's brush: he used a cold white, which blended with a layer of ochre shining through from below and resulted in that grey tone which is also found in the late pictures of Frans Hals. Rembrandt refused to adopt the light, clear colours that had now become fashionable and he continued to cling to his convictions. The fatal results of that attitude can be seen in what happened to a large picture commissioned from him in the early 1660s for the new Town Hall of Amsterdam.

This painting, the *Conspiracy of Julius Civilis: the Oath*, is now a fragment (Plate 91). The original composition, which is known from a small sketch, showed a group of men, the Batavians, assembled round a large table in a huge vaulted hall. The architectural setting was veiled in darkness and only the central group of conspirators stood out in brilliant light; they are bathed in glowing gold, which submerges all other colours. Contrary to every classical ideal, the figures are robust and thickset, their gestures abrupt and angular. Nor did Rembrandt hesitate to make clear that the leader of the conspiracy, Julius Civilis, had lost one eye. This disregard for decorum and the uncompromising style must have shocked the city officials: they declared the picture to be a failure and refused to accept it.

The last years of Rembrandt's life were overshadowed by tragedy: Hendrickje died in 1663 and Titus in 1668; only Hendrickje's daughter Cornelia survived him. But during those years he created some of his greatest masterpieces. The *Jewish Bride* (Plate 26), a picture in which portraiture is inextricably linked with a Biblical theme, shows a young couple, perhaps Jacob and Rachel. The infinitely tender gesture of the hands, gently touching before the woman's breast, is most moving. The man and the woman look neither at one another nor at the spectator: they gaze into their souls, into a world of deepest peace and trust, with the merest suggestion of an almost invisible smile. In the work of Rembrandt, love and peace have found their consummate pictorial expression.

The '*Syndics*', depicting the sampling officials of the clothmakers' guild (Plate 22), looks somewhat more conservative than Rembrandt's other late paintings. It is hardly bolder than the late group portraits of Frans Hals. Perhaps Rembrandt was unwilling in this instance to jeopardize the success of the commission, and the two inscribed dates, 1661 and 1662, might suggest that the board of the clothmakers' guild demanded some changes in the picture after it was delivered. In any event, the problem presented by a group portrait has here been solved with conspicuous success. The composition recalls the *Regents of the St Elizabeth Hospital* by Hals, but none of Rembrandt's sitters turns his back to the spectator; all of them look out of the picture, and one is even about to rise as if to greet an unexpected visitor. The spectator can imagine that he is himself the visitor, and thus the somewhat forced compromise between action and portrait which one senses in Hals's picture has here been avoided.

In the *Return of the Prodigal Son* (Plate 27) Rembrandt's religious fervour reached its most intense and moving expression. He had drawn close to the Dutch Mennonites, whose beliefs placed special emphasis on God's readiness to forgive the repentant sinner, and his picture exalts human goodness and Christian mercy. The father's gesture of forgiveness, as he protectively shelters his ragged son, places this picture, like the *Jewish Bride*, among the most eloquent and unforgettable in Rembrandt's work.

The rendering of human emotions is one of the great themes which occupied him throughout his creative career. His drawings and etchings reveal the same continuous search for ever more expressive gestures and features. The letter which Rembrandt wrote to Constantijn Huygens about the Passion series, mentioned earlier, shows us that Rembrandt was consciously pursuing this aim. In his middle period he had tried to reach it by using the dramatic means of the International Baroque style; in his later work there is an intensified concentration on ever more economical gestures or even mere suggestions. Here the states of mind are conveyed by the portrayal of solitary figures who find peace within themselves or who feel threatened by the ambivalence of their feelings. The distribution of light can also play a part in this psychological exploration: in some paintings it condemns the figures to cruel isolation, in others it protects them like a luminous shield. Rembrandt's self-scrutiny in his self-portraits (Plates 78, 79) documents, on a more limited scale, the same stylistic developments which have here been briefly sketched.

One of the essential differences between the work of Hals, Vermeer and Rembrandt was the degree of specialization. Rembrandt dominated Dutch painting of his age partly because of his versatility, his mastery of portraiture, landscape, Biblical and mythological illustration and his virtuosity in the media of painting, etching and drawing. Hals and Vermeer, on the other hand, were first and foremost painters of portraits and domestic interiors respectively. In a small country that supported an incredible number of artists, specialization was a basic necessity, the safest means of establishing a sharp enough professional identity to survive and prosper.

This book illustrates most of the specialized forms that made up the pattern of seventeenth-century Dutch painting. Flower painting is represented by Rachel Ruysch (Plate 96), one of the last of the masters in this important and popular genre. Of the still-life painters, Willem Kalf was undoubtedly the greatest, and the *Still Life with Nautilus Cup* (Plate 93) is highly characteristic in the way in which elaborate, even ostentatious subject matter is both controlled and enhanced by the delicacy of Kalf's observation. The gleams of reflected light on the platter, the highlights on the Oriental bowl and the tight juicy texture of the unpeeled lemon are almost worthy of Vermeer.

The Dutch, denied religious art in their churches because of the Protestant ethic, developed an extraordinary appetite for pictures of their own world. Landscape painting flourished as never before. From its humble beginnings in the art of Esaias van de Velde (Plates 1, 44) and Hercules Seghers (Plate 48), and its evolving mastery in the subtle, tonal painting of Jan van Goyen (Plate 2), landscape reached its highest point in the sombre and majestic canvases of Jacob van Ruisdael (Plates 28, 29, 53). Ruisdael's mastery of naturalistic effects, however, above all his delineation of overcast skies pierced by rays of fleeting sunshine, should never blind one to the basic artifice of his work. He did not simply paint what he saw. He rearranged facts and features of nature so as to create a heightened mood, both sombre and powerful. This is particularly apparent in one of his most celebrated compositions, the *Cemetery* (Plate 65), which so impressed the great German writer, Goethe, and the German Romantic painter, Caspar David Friedrich.

There were other important landscape painters. Hendrick Avercamp was the first Dutch artist of talent to depict Dutch landscape, which formed the backgrounds to his winter scenes full of gay crowds (Plate 37). He was followed by such interesting artists as Aert van der Neer (Plate 16), in whose winter and moonlit scenes light effects played an essential part and inspired such masters as Jan van de Cappelle; Meyndert Hobbema, whose woodland pictures (Plates 30, 84) approach perfection; Aelbert Cuyp (Plate 19), whose mastery of sunlight made him one of the most popular of Dutch masters with English collectors in the late eighteenth and early nineteenth centuries; and Jan van der Heyden, whose meticulous townscapes (Plates 4, 85) give one a remarkably clear-sighted yet affectionate image of what many of the smaller towns and cities of Holland actually looked like.

Closely related to landscape painting was another artform very popular in seventeenth-century Holland: marine painting. Among its most brilliant exponents were Simon de Vlieger (Plate 14), Salomon van Ruysdael (Plate 13) and Jan van de Cappelle (Plates 17, 58). Willem van de Velde the younger (Plate 59) became the best-known sea painter and was enthusiastically received in England when he and his father became painters to Charles II in the 1670s.

Biographical Notes

Hendrick Avercamp (1585–1634)
Born in Amsterdam, Hendrick Avercamp spent most of his life in Campen. He painted outdoor winter scenes filled with crowds of animated people. His early works are reminiscent of Pieter Bruegel but more realistic. He was dumb and was called 'de stomme van Kampen' (the mute from Campen). His style was followed by his nephew and pupil Barent Avercamp and influenced the works of Jan van Goyen and Aert van der Neer among others. He died in Campen, aged 49.
Plate 37

Gerrit Berckheyde (1638–1698)
Born in Haarlem, Gerrit Berckheyde learned painting from his elder brother Job. He specialized in townscapes, and painted realistic views of every major Dutch town. The market place in Haarlem was a subject he painted many times. In 1660 he joined the painters' guild in Haarlem, where he died in 1698.
Plate 5

Gerard ter Borch (1617–1681)
Born in Zwolle, Gerard ter Borch was the son of an artist who was probably also his first teacher. He travelled to England, France, Germany, Spain and Italy. He was a master of detail, lovingly reproducing the textures of delicate porcelain, embroidery, fur and satin. He began by painting soldiers but soon turned to small portraits of the burgher class. It was after he settled in Deventer in 1654 that he concentrated on his brilliant scenes of contemporary life, painted in a new and individual style. He died in Deventer.
Plates 57, 72 and 88

Adriaen Brouwer (about 1606–1638)
Born in Oudenaarde, in Flanders, Adriaen Brouwer may have been a pupil of Frans Hals in Haarlem sometime between 1620 and 1624. Despite the fact that he was born in Flanders and spent part of his life there, he is often considered a painter of the Dutch school. He specialized in peasant scenes, and his approach was as frank and direct as that of Hals. His brilliant characterizations of free-living peasants—his favourite subjects—are appealing in their spontaneity; the poverty of the surroundings is made vivid by the richness of his colours and technique. Rubens and Rembrandt were admirers and collectors of his work. He was said to be aged 32 when he died, bankrupt, in Antwerp.
Plates 41 and 71

Hendrick ter Brugghen (1588?–1629)
Very little is known about Hendrick ter Brugghen's early years, but he was probably born in Deventer. He is known to have visited Italy between 1604 and 1614, where he may have been personally acquainted with Caravaggio, by whose works he was strongly influenced. He settled in Utrecht, joined the painters' guild in 1616 and continued to follow Caravaggio's style, which appealed to and was imitated by most of the Utrecht artists. Typical works by ter Brugghen are large portraits of half-length figures, with brilliant colours and surprising light effects. He died in Utrecht.
Plate 38

Jan van de Cappelle (about 1624–1679)
Little is known about Jan van de Cappelle's early life. He was born in Amsterdam, the son of a master dyer, and is said to have been self-taught. A man of wealth, he collected a large number of paintings and drawings, including some 500 drawings by Rembrandt and 1,300 drawings by Simon de Vlieger, who influenced his early work. Perhaps the greatest Dutch marine painter, he also painted winter landscapes, inspired no doubt by Aert van der Neer. His delicate atmospheric studies of the sea are closely related to those of Aelbert Cuyp. Van de Cappelle died in Amsterdam.
Plates 17 and 58

Aelbert Cuyp (1620–1691)
Son of a painter, Aelbert Cuyp was born in Dordrecht, where he spent all of his life. Although one of the great Dutch landscape painters, he was remarkably versatile, his oeuvre including portraits, still lifes and townscapes. His early landscapes were influenced by Jan van Goyen.

The amazing luminosity of his river and sea scenes is reminiscent of van de Cappelle's paintings. He is perhaps best remembered for his lovely and peaceful landscapes, bathed in golden sunlight and scattered with cows. Cuyp married well in 1658 and died in Dordrecht at the age of 71.
Plate 19

Gerrit Dou (1613–1675)
Born in Leyden, Gerrit (sometimes spelled Gerard) Dou was the son of a glass engraver. He learned his father's trade and became a member of the glaziers' guild. When he was fourteen he began studying under Rembrandt, with whom he spent three years. He was one of the first members of the painters' guild in Leyden and enjoyed enormous popularity as a painter of realistic genre scenes. A favourite technique of his was to portray the face of his sitter lit by a candle from an inner room or window sill. His meticulous attention to detail won him many admirers and imitators, including Frans van Mieris and Gabriel Metsu. He was invited by Charles II to work for him in England but he refused, preferring to remain in Leyden, where he died.
Plate 63

Allart van Everdingen (1621–1675)
Born at Alkamaar, Allart van Everdingen was the younger brother of Cesar van Everdingen. He travelled to Scandinavia in 1644, a trip that influenced his landscapes for the rest of his life. The Scandinavian motifs that he introduced—mountains, waterfalls, rocks, stately firs—became popular with Dutch artists and influenced Jacob van Ruisdael. Everdingen lived in Haarlem from 1645 until at least 1651, and it was there that he married and joined the painters' guild. He later moved to Amsterdam and died there.
Plate 15

Carel Fabritius (1622–1654)
Born in Midden-Beemster, Carel Pietersz. was the son of a schoolmaster. He trained as a carpenter and adopted Fabritius as a surname (*faber* in Latin means a worker in hard materials) before he became a pupil of Rembrandt. He married between 1641 and 1643 and had two children, but lost his wife and both children. He married again in 1650 and spent the last few years of his life in Delft. He was fascinated by perspective and light effects, passing on both these interests to Vermeer, who was probably his pupil. Fabritius was one of the most gifted painters in Holland in the seventeenth century and strongly influenced genre painting in Delft. His life was tragically cut short in the explosion of a powder magazine in Delft in 1654.
Plate 36

Jan van Goyen (1596–1656)
Born in Leyden, Jan van Goyen was one of the greatest of the Dutch landscape painters. He was the pupil of several masters. He travelled in France for a year, 1616–17, before going to Haarlem to study under Esaias van de Velde, who was a strong influence on his early work. Van Goyen probably returned to Leyden in 1618, the year he married. In the 1620s his development corresponded closely to that of Pieter de Molijn and Salomon van Ruysdael, who were also working in Haarlem. Sometime about 1630 his style changed and was characterized by much greater simplicity; his landscapes were no longer crowded with figures and details, and he used lighter, softer colours. His art was imitated by many other landscape painters. One of his pupils was Jan Steen, who married van Goyen's daughter in 1649. Van Goyen died in The Hague at the age of 60.
Plate 2

Frans Hals (about 1580–1666)
Little is known about Frans Hals's early years. He was probably born in Antwerp but lived in Haarlem from 1585 onwards. He may have been a pupil of Karel van Mander and in 1610 joined the painters' guild. His first wife died in 1615 and in 1617 he remarried. He had at least ten children, several of whom became painters. Although he received a number of commissions for portraits, including group portraits for militia companies, he was nevertheless always in financial difficulties. Among the distinguished artists said to have been taught by him are Adriaen Brouwer, Adriaen van Ostade and Judith Leyster. The last two years of his life he received a pension from the town council of Haarlem. He died and was buried in Haarlem.
Plates 7–12, 23, 39, 43, 46, 47, 67, 70 and 94

Jan van der Heyden (1637–1712)
Born in Gorinchem, by 1650 Jan van der Heyden was

in Amsterdam, where he lived the rest of his life. He was trained by a glass painter. Although he painted landscapes and still lifes, his most famous and most frequent works were townscapes. His love was architecture, and he painted not only topographical scenes, but architectural fantasies. His technique, though more meticulous, is similar to de Hoogh's. Besides painting, he invented improvements in street lighting and fire fighting; he is said to have invented the fire hose, on which he published a monograph in 1690. It is apparent from his work that he travelled fairly extensively. He died in Amsterdam.
Plates 4 and 85

Meyndert Hobbema (1638–1709)

Born in Amsterdam, Meyndert Hobbema was taught by Jacob van Ruisdael, who was the major influence on his work. Hobbema lacked the versatility of his great master, and his landscapes do not have the same deep, poetic quality, but they are nevertheless brilliant achievements. In virtually all of his works trees play an important part. His free, spontaneous style was much admired by the Impressionists in the nineteenth century, when Hobbema was rediscovered after many years of relative obscurity. He painted very little after his marriage in 1668, when he became a wine gauger in Amsterdam. He died in Amsterdam at the age of 71.
Plates 30 and 84

Pieter de Hoogh (1629–after 1684)

Born in Rotterdam, Pieter de Hoogh (sometimes spelt de Hooch) became one of the greatest Dutch genre painters. He was the son of a stonemason and was a pupil of Nicolaes Berchem, presumably in Haarlem. He was in the service of a cloth merchant in 1653, when he is recorded to have arrived in Delft. He married the daughter of a Delft faience painter the following year and joined the painters' guild. He was influenced by Fabritius and Vermeer, both of whom were active in Delft. His subjects were interiors and courtyard scenes, all of which give us a picture of middleclass life in Holland in the seventeenth century. His concern was not with the people in his paintings so much as with the space; it was perspective and spatial shapes that fascinated him. De Hoogh moved to Amsterdam in 1666, after which time his artistic development deteriorated sharply.

There are works dated 1684, but it is not known where or when he died.
Plates 56 and 83

Willem Kalf (1619–1693)

One of the greatest Dutch still-life painters, Willem Kalf was born in Rotterdam. He was influenced by Rembrandt, whose chiaroscuro technique he imitated, and Vermeer, whose blue-yellow harmony Kalf favoured. His typical still lifes portray precious porcelain and glass, rich Persian rugs and exotic fruits, placed against a dark background. He married Cornelia Fluvier, a talented poet and diamond engraver, at Hoorn in 1651, and two years later settled in Amsterdam, where he spent the rest of his life.
Plate 93

Philips Koninck (1619–1688)

Born in Amsterdam, Philips Koninck was taught painting by his elder brother, Jacob, in Rotterdam. He may also have been a pupil of Rembrandt, whose Biblical scenes and landscapes were strong influences on Koninck's works. He was also influenced by Hercules Seghers. His landscapes are usually viewed from a high vantage point, and there is a clear separation between land and sky; depth is achieved through his arrangement of the landscape elements, with a winding river or road often taking the spectator into the distance. Koninck married in Amsterdam in 1642 and died there in 1688.
Plate 45

Gabriel Metsu (1629–1667)

Born in Leyden, Gabriel Metsu became a popular genre painter. He probably studied under Gerrit Dou and, like Dou, was one of the founder members of the painters' guild in Leyden in 1648. By 1657 he had moved to Amsterdam. His interiors show the influence of Vermeer, and although they cannot compare with that great master's works, Metsu was nevertheless a gifted painter. He married in 1658 in Amsterdam and died there at the age of 38.
Plate 89

Frans van Mieris (1635–1681)

Born in Leyden, Frans van Mieris (the elder) was the son of a goldsmith. He was the most important pupil of Gerrit Dou, who clearly influenced his work. Van

Mieris specialized in portraits and small genre scenes. He was a popular artist, visited by Cosimo of Tuscany in 1667. He spent his life in Leyden, where he was made dean of the painters' guild in 1665. Among the many artists who imitated his work were his sons, Jan and Willem. Van Mieris died in Leyden.
Plate 73

Aernout (Aert) van der Neer (1603/4–1677)

Aert van der Neer worked as a steward with a family in Gorinchem before he moved to Amsterdam in the early 1630s and became a painter. It is not known whether he was taught painting. Most of his paintings are moonlit landscapes and winter scenes, in which he brilliantly explored the effects of evening light and reflections on snow. His work inspired Jan van de Cappelle. Van der Neer kept an inn in Amsterdam from 1659 to 1662, when he was declared bankrupt. His last years were spent in poverty in Amstedam.
Plate 16

Adriaen van Ostade (1610–1685)

Born in Haarlem, Adriaen van Ostade was a painter and etcher of peasant scenes. He is said to have been taught by Frans Hals although he seems to have been much more influenced by Adriaen Brouwer, who may also have been a pupil of Hals. His early works—gay and amusing scenes of drinking peasants—are very much like Brouwer's, although less dramatic and powerful; his later paintings, equally charming, are more respectable. He married, secondly, a wealthy woman, and became dean of the painters' guild in Haarlem, where he died aged 74. His work was popular and attracted many contemporary forgers.
Plate 61

Isack van Ostade (1621–1649)

The younger brother and pupil of Adriaen van Ostade, Isack van Ostade was born in Haarlem. His early work, influenced by his brother, was mainly peasant genre. But his more important paintings were his landscapes, particularly his winter scenes, in which he incorporated his interest in genre by portraying figures. He died when he was only 28, in Haarlem.
Plate 52

Paulus Potter (1625–1654)

Son of a painter, Paulus Potter was born at Enkhuizen. Almost all of his paintings are of animals—usually grazing cattle, horses or sheep—in landscape. He also made many etchings and sketches of animals. His work was popular and he attracted imitators well into the nineteenth century. He lived in Delft, The Hague (where he married in 1650) and finally in Amsterdam, where he died when he was only 28.
Plate 18

Rembrandt (1606–1669)

Born in Leyden, Rembrandt Harmensz. van Rijn was the son of a miller. For a short time he attended Leyden University and after studying painting—first in Leyden under Jacob van Swanenburgh and then in Amsterdam with Pieter Lastman—he set up on his own as a painter. In 1628 Gerrit Dou became his pupil and stayed with him for about three years. By July 1632 Rembrandt had moved to Amsterdam, where he lived in the house of an art-dealer, Hendrick van Uylenburgh, whose niece, Saskia, Rembrandt married two years later. The next eight years were happy and very successful ones: he received many commissions, lived well and built up a large art collection. In 1642 Saskia died. His popularity declined somewhat and he fell deeply into debt. He was supported by Hendrickje Stoffels, with whom he lived from about 1645 until her death in 1668, and his son Titus. He was survived only by his illegitimate daughter when he died, in extreme poverty, in Amsterdam, aged 63.
Plates 22, 24–27, 42, 49–51, 55, 64, 66, 68, 69, 74, 75, 78, 79, 87, 90 and 91

Jacob van Ruisdael (1628/9?–1682)

The greatest of the Dutch landscape painters, Jacob van Ruisdael was born in Haarlem, probably in 1628 or 1629. His father, a frame-maker and art-dealer, is thought to have painted landscapes and probably taught his son to paint. Jacob may also have been a pupil of his uncle, Salomon van Ruysdael, whose influence is apparent in his early works. But Ruisdael soon developed his own style, and his landscape masterpieces illustrate a unique ability to convey mood, poetry and spiritual depth. He joined the Haarlem guild in 1648 but by 1657 had settled

in Amsterdam, where he probably died. He was buried in Haarlem.
Plates 28, 29, 53 and 65

Rachel Ruysch (1664–1750)

Born in Amsterdam in 1664, Rachel Ruysch was a popular floral painter. Her still lifes, usually of flowers, sometimes of fruit, are carefully arranged compositions, generally with a dark background. She married a minor painter and had ten children. From 1708 to 1713 she was court painter at Düsseldorf. She died in Amsterdam.
Plate 96

Salomon van Ruysdael (1600/3–1670)

Born at Naarden in Gooiland, Salomon van Ruysdael was the uncle and perhaps the teacher of Jacob van Ruisdael. He was one of the most important of the early Dutch landscape painters and was influenced by Esaias van de Velde. Ruysdael's early style was closely related to that of van Goyen. He lived all his life in Haarlem, where he joined the painters' guild in 1623.
Plate 13

Pieter Saenredam (1597–1665)

Born at Assendelft, Pieter Saenredam was the son of an engraver. He went to Haarlem as a child, became a pupil of Frans Pietersz. de Grebber, portrait and history painter, in 1612, and stayed with him for ten years. In 1623 he joined the painters' guild in Haarlem, of which he was later made secretary, steward and dean. He specialized in church interiors and architectural views, all of which illustrate his fascination with—and good grasp of—perspective. His earliest known work is his illustrations to a history of Haarlem written by Samuel Ampzing and published in 1628. Saenredam died in Haarlem.
Plate 3

Hercules Seghers (1589/90–after January 1633)

Details of Hercules Segher's life are sketchy. He was born in Haarlem, and was a pupil of Gillis van Coninxloo. He was one of the most important early Dutch landscape painters and had perhaps the greatest single influence on the development of landscape painting in Holland. His paintings and etchings were widely known to his contemporaries and inspired, among others, Rembrandt (also a collector of his pictures) and Philips

Koninck. He joined the painters' guild in Haarlem in 1612, but had moved to Amsterdam by 1614 and The Hague by January 1633, after which date there is no record of him.
Plate 48

Jan Steen (1625/6–1679)

One of the great Dutch painters, Jan Steen, son of a brewer, was born in Leyden. He is said to have been a pupil of Adriaen van Ostade and Jan van Goyen, whose daughter he married in 1649. He specialized in scenes of contemporary life, and although usually humorous, they were also, on a deeper level, shrewd moral comments on life. His genius in painting genre was not matched by any of his contemporaries. He lived in The Hague, Leyden and perhaps briefly in Delft before settling in Haarlem in 1661. In 1670 he inherited a house in Leyden, where he lived until his death.
Plates 20, 21, 40 and 62

Esaias van de Velde (about 1590–1630)

Son of a painter, Esaias van de Velde was born in Amsterdam. He may have been a pupil of Gillis van Coninxloo. Van de Velde and Hercules Seghers both joined the painters' guild in Haarlem in 1612 and both played a decisive role in the development of Dutch landscape painting. Van de Velde taught Jan van Goyen, and was a strong influence on him and many other landscape painters. In 1618 he moved to The Hague, where he died.
Plates 1 and 44

Willem van de Velde the younger (1633–1707)

Son of the marine artist Willem van de Velde the elder, who was also his first teacher, Willem the younger was born in Leyden. He is thought to have been a pupil of Simon de Vlieger, whose influence can be seen in van de Velde's early work. Van de Velde became the leading marine painter, enjoying wide popularity in Holland and in England, where he and his father lived from 1672. They were taken into the service of Charles II and remained at the English court for the rest of their lives, making brief visits to Holland. After his move to England Willem the younger painted fewer seascapes and concentrated more on specific vessels and naval events. He is buried at St James's, Piccadilly.
Plate 59

Johannes Vermeer (1632–1675)
The son of a silk-weaver and innkeeper, Johannes Vermeer was born in Delft. Little is known about his artistic training but he seems to have been influenced by Carel Fabritius, who had joined the painters' guild in Delft the year before Vermeer joined in 1653. His work also indicates a knowledge of the Utrecht followers of Caravaggio; this influence is evident in Vermeer's earliest dated work, the *Procuress* of 1656. He gained fame in his lifetime but was often in debt. He dealt in works of art but seems to have sold few of his own; his wife inherited 29 of his paintings when he died. Today fewer than 40 can be attributed to him. He was in debt when he died in Delft, aged 43.
Plates 6, 31–35, 77, 80–82, 86, 92 and 95

Johannes Cornelisz. Verspronck (1597–1642)
Born in Haarlem, Johannes Cornelisz. Verspronck was a successful portrait painter. He was a pupil of Frans Hals. He died in Haarlem.
Plate 54

Simon de Vlieger (about 1600–1653)
Born in Rotterdam, Simon de Vlieger was an important seascape painter. He played a large part in the development of marine painting, and his style was reflected in the paintings of Jan van de Cappelle (who owned 1,300 of Vlieger's drawings as well as some of his paintings) and Willem van de Velde the younger, who was probably his pupil. He made many etchings of animals and landscapes as well as seascapes. He married in Rotterdam in 1627, and later lived in Delft, Amsterdam and Weesp, where he died.
Plate 14

Emanuel de Witte (1615/17–1691/2)
Born in Alkmaar, Emanuel de Witte became a member of the painters' guild there in 1636. He moved to Rotterdam, then to Delft, and probably settled in Amsterdam in 1651. He is said to have been taught by a still-life painter, although his earliest known pictures are portraits. After 1650 he specialized in church interiors but also painted domestic and market scenes, sometimes with portraits. He drank and was frequently in debt, often painting for people in return for his keep; He was found early in 1692 in a frozen Amsterdam canal, eleven weeks after he had disappeared; he was suspected to have committed suicide.
Plates 60 and 76

List of Plates

BLACK AND WHITE PLATES

1. Esaias van de Velde (*c. 1590–1630*). *A Winter Scene.* 1614. Panel, 25·5 × 32 cm. Raleigh, North Carolina, Museum of Art

2. Jan van Goyen (1596–1656). *Landscape with a Tavern.* 1646. Panel, 36 × 62 cm. Paris, Musée du Petit-Palais

3. Pieter Saenredam (1597–1665). *Old Town Hall, Amsterdam.* 1657. Panel, 64·5 × 83 cm. Amsterdam, Rijksmuseum

4. Jan van der Heyden (1637–1712). *New Town Hall, Amsterdam.* Canvas, 72 × 86 cm. Paris, Louvre

5. Gerrit Berckheyde (1638–98). *The Flower Market in Amsterdam.* Canvas, 45 × 61 cm. Amsterdam, Rijksmuseum.

6. Johannes Vermeer (1632–75). *View of Delft.* About 1660. Canvas, 98·5 × 117·5 cm. The Hague, Mauritshuis

7. Frans Hals (1580?–1666). *Laughing Boy with a Jug.* About 1626–8. Canvas, 69·5 × 58 cm. Rotterdam, Boymans-van Beuningen Museum (on loan from the Hofje van Aerden, Leerdam)

8. Frans Hals (1580?–1666). *Gipsy Girl.* About 1628–30. Panel, 58 × 52 cm. Paris, Louvre

9. Frans Hals (1580?–1666). *Willem van Heythuyzen.* About 1637–9. Panel, 46·5 × 37·5 cm. Brussels, Musée Royal des Beaux-Arts

10. Frans Hals (1580?–1666). *Jonker Ramp and his Sweetheart.* 1623. Canvas mounted on panel, 105·5 × 79 cm. New York, The Metropolitan Museum of Art

11. Frans Hals (1580?–1666). *Banquet of the Officers of the St Hadrian Militia Company.* About 1627. Canvas, 183 × 266·5 cm. Haarlem, Frans Hals Museum

12. Frans Hals (1580?–1666). *Banquet of the Officers of the St George Militia Company.* About 1627. Canvas, 179 × 257·5 cm. Haarlem, Frans Hals Museum

13. Salomon van Ruysdael (1600/3–1670). *Coast with Fish-carts.* 1635(?). Panel, 34 × 55 cm. Whereabouts unknown

14. Simon de Vlieger (*c. 1600–1653*). *Beach near Scheveningen.* 1633. Panel, 68 × 106 cm. Greenwich, National Maritime Museum

15. Allart van Everdingen (1621–75). *Snowstorm at Sea.* Canvas, 97 × 121 cm. Chantilly, Musée Condé

16. Aert van der Neer (1603/4–1677). *Frozen River.* Canvas, 64 × 79 cm. Amsterdam, Rijksmuseum

17. Jan van de Cappelle (*c. 1624–1679*). *Bridge across a Frozen Canal.* 1653. Canvas, 52 × 62 cm. The Hague, Mauritshuis

18. Paulus Potter (1625–54). *Cows Reflected in the Water.* 1648. Panel, 44 × 61·5 cm. The Hague, Mauritshuis

19. Aelbert Cuyp (1620–91). *The Avenue at Meerdervoort, Dordrecht.* About 1660–5. Canvas, 70 × 98 cm. London, Wallace Collection

20. Jan Steen (1625/6–1679). *Grace before Meat.* About 1665. Canvas, 45 × 37·5 cm. London, National Gallery

21. Jan Steen (1625/6–1679). *The Dissolute Family.* Canvas, 63·5 × 51 cm. Private Collection

22. Rembrandt (1606–69). *The Sampling Officials of the Clothmakers' Guild, Amsterdam ('The Syndics').* 1661/2. Canvas, 191 × 279 cm. Amsterdam, Rijksmuseum

23. Frans Hals (1580?–1666). *Regents of the Old Men's Alms House.* About 1664. Canvas, 172·5 × 256 cm. Haarlem, Frans Hals Museum

24. Rembrandt (1606–69). *Portrait of Jan Six.* 1654. Canvas, 112 × 102 cm. Amsterdam, Six Collection

25. Rembrandt (1606–69). *The Anatomy Lesson of Dr Nicolaes Tulp.* 1632. Canvas, 169·5 × 216·5 cm. The Hague, Mauritshuis

26. Rembrandt (1606–69). *The Jewish Bride.* After 1665. Canvas, 121·5 × 166·5 cm. Amsterdam, Rijksmuseum

27. Rembrandt (1606–69). *The Return of the Prodigal Son.* About 1668–9. Canvas, 262 × 206 cm. Leningrad, Hermitage

28. Jacob van Ruisdael (1628/9?–1682). *Castle of Bentheim.* Canvas, 68 × 54 cm. Amsterdam, Rijksmuseum

29. Jacob van Ruisdael (1628/9?–1682). *A Landscape with a Ruined Castle and a Church.* Canvas, 109 × 146 cm. London, National Gallery

Colour Plates

37 *Hendrick Avercamp*. A Winter Landscape. *Detail. Cologne, Wallraf–Richartz Museum*

38 *Hendrick ter Brugghen.* The Flute Player. *1621. Kassel, Gemäldegalerie*

39 *Frans Hals*. Pieter van den Broecke. *About 1633. London, Kenwood House, Iveagh Bequest*

40 *Jan Steen*. Self-Portrait with Lute. *About 1662. Lugano–Castagnola, Thyssen–Bornemisza Collection*

41 *Adriaen Brouwer.* The·Performance. *About 1630. Munich, Alte Pinakothek*

42 *Rembrandt.* The Artist's Mother(?). *About 1629/30. London, Royal Collection*

43 *Frans Hals.* Nurse and Child. *About 1620. Berlin–Dahlem, Staatliche Museen*

44 *Esaias van de Velde.* A Winter Landscape. *1623. London, National Gallery*

45 *Philips Koninck*. View with Cottages by the Roadside. *1676. Amsterdam, Rijksmuseum*

46 *Frans Hals*. Ensign Adriaen Marham. *Detail from the St Hadrian Militia Company portrait of 1627 (Plate 11)*

47 *Frans Hals.* Captain Nicolaes Verbeeck. *Detail from the St George Militia Company portrait of
1627 (Plate 12)*

48 *Hercules Seghers*. A River Valley with a Group of Houses. *About 1625. Rotterdam, Boymans–van Beuningen Museum*

49 *Rembrandt*. The Risen Christ and Mary Magdalene at the Tomb. *1638. London, Royal Collection*

50 *Rembrandt*. Belshazzar's Feast. *About 1635. London, National Gallery*

51 *Rembrandt. Uzziah Stricken with Leprosy(?). 1635. Chatsworth, Derbyshire, The Trustees of the Chatsworth Settlement*

52 *Isack van Ostade*. A Winter Scene. *About 1645. London, National Gallery*

53 *Jacob van Ruisdael.* The Mill at Wijk bij Duurstede. *About 1670. Amsterdam, Rijksmuseum*

54 *Johannes Cornelisz. Verspronck. Portrait of a Girl in a Blue Dress. 1641. Amsterdam, Rijksmuseum*

55 *Rembrandt. Detail from* The Militia Company of Captain Frans Banning Cocq ('The Night Watch'). *1642. Amsterdam, Rijksmuseum. Complete picture illustrated right*

56 *Pieter de Hoogh*. Woman Sewing, with Child. *Lugano-Castagnola, Thyssen-Bornemisza Collection*

57 *Gerard ter Borch*. The Letter. *1660. London, Royal Collection*

58 *Jan van de Cappelle.* The State Barge Saluted by the Home Fleet. *Detail. 1650. Amsterdam, Rijksmuseum*

59 *Willem van de Velde the younger*. The Cannon Shot. *About 1670. Amsterdam, Rijksmuseum*

60 *Emanuel de Witte*. Adriana van Heusden and her Daughter at the New Fishmarket in Amsterdam(?). *About 1661–3. London, National Gallery*

61 *Adriaen van Ostade.* An Alchemist. *1661. London, National Gallery*

62 *Jan Steen.* The Lovesick Girl. *Prague, National Gallery*

63 *Gerrit Dou*. Woman with Dropsy. *1663. Paris, Louvre*

64 *Rembrandt.* The Entombment of Christ. *1636–8(?). Glasgow University, Hunterian Museum*

65 *Jacob van Ruisdael*. The Cemetery. *Detroit Institute of Arts*

66 *Rembrandt.* Portrait of the Painter Hendrick Martensz. Sorgh. *1647. Private Collection*

67 *Frans Hals*. Portrait of a Man. *About 1650–2. New York, The Metropolitan Museum of Art*

68 *Rembrandt*. Portrait of Titus. *1655. Rotterdam, Boymans–van Beuningen Museum*

69 *Rembrandt.* Aristotle Contemplating a Bust of Homer. *1653. New York, The Metropolitan Museum of Art*

70 *Frans Hals.* Portrait of a Seated Man Holding a Branch. *Detail. About 1645. Ottawa, National Gallery of Canada*

71 *Adriaen Brouwer.* Portrait of a Man in a Pointed Hat. *About 1630. Rotterdam, Boymans–van Beuningen Museum*

72 *Gerard ter Borch*. The Introduction. *About 1662. Polesden Lacey, The National Trust*

73 *Frans van Mieris*. Amorous Scene. *1658. The Hague, Mauritshuis*

74 *Rembrandt.* The Presentation of Jesus in the Temple. *1631. The Hague, Mauritshuis*

75 *Rembrandt*. Christ and the Woman taken in Adultery. *1644. London, National Gallery*

76 *Emanuel de Witte*. Interior of the New Church in Delft. *1656. Lille, Musée des Beaux-Arts*

77 *Johannes Vermeer*. A Street in Delft. *About 1659. Amsterdam, Rijksmuseum*

78 *Rembrandt.* Self–Portrait. *About 1639. Los Angeles, Norton Simon Collection*

79 *Rembrandt*. Self–Portrait as the Apostle Paul. *1661. Amsterdam, Rijksmuseum*

80 *Johannes Vermeer.* The Lacemaker. *About 1665. Paris, Louvre*

81 *Johannes Vermeer.* Lady Weighing Pearls. *Detail from Plate 32*

82 *Johannes Vermeer*. A Painter in his Studio. *About 1666. Vienna, Kunsthistorisches Museum*

83 *Pieter de Hoogh*. At the Linen Cupboard. *1663. Amsterdam, Rijksmuseum*

84 *Meyndert Hobbema*. The Watermill. *1670. Chicago, Art Institute*

85 *Jan van der Heyden*. Approach to the Town of Veere. *About 1665. London, Royal Collection*

86 *Johannes Vermeer*. Christ in the House of Mary and Martha. *About 1654. Edinburgh, National Gallery of Scotland*

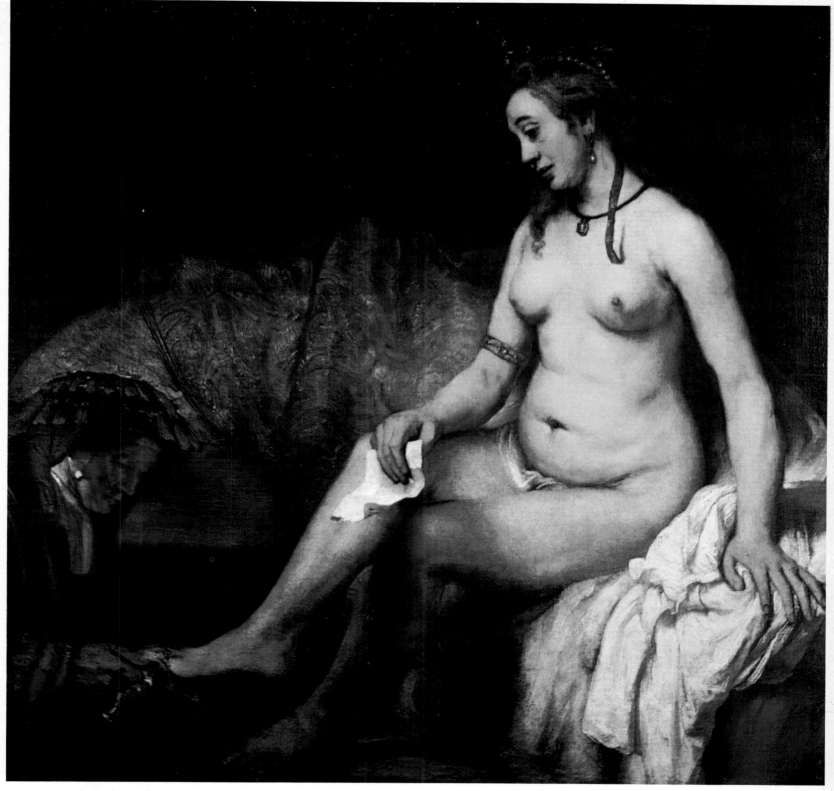

87 *Rembrandt.* Bathsheba with King David's Letter. *1654. Paris, Louvre*

88 *Gerard ter Borch*. Mother Ridding her Child of Lice. *1650–3. The Hague, Mauritshuis*

89 *Gabriel Metsu.* The Sick Child. *About 1660. Amsterdam, Rijksmuseum*

90 *Rembrandt. Detail from* Belshazzar's Feast *(Plate 50)*

91 *Rembrandt. Detail from* The Conspiracy of Julius Civilis: the Oath. *1661. Stockholm, Nationalmuseum. Whole of surviving fragment illustrated right*

92 *Johannes Vermeer*. The Procuress. *1656. Dresden, Gemäldegalerie*

93 *Willem Kalf.* Still Life with Nautilus Cup. *1662. Lugano-Castagnola,*
Thyssen-Bornemisza Collection

94 *Frans Hals*. Portrait of a Seated Woman. *Detail. About 1660. Oxford, Christ Church*

95 *Johannes Vermeer*. Young Lady with a Pearl Necklace. *Detail from Plate 34*

96 *Rachel Ruysch*. Roses, Marigolds, Hyacinth and other Flowers on a Marble Ledge. *1723*.
Glasgow, *Art Gallery and Museum*